A journey through

YORKSHIRE

JARROLD

YORKSHIRE

Yorkshire is England's largest county, despite the administrative alterations to its borders in recent times. More than 1,000 years ago the Danes divided it into three parts ('tredings') which gave us the three 'ridings' we know today. This book, loosely based on the ancient divisions, is divided into northern, western and southern Yorkshire, but it does not cover Humberside or Cleveland, which are independent areas in their own right.

The variety of landscape within Yorkshire is immense. There is pastoral, agricultural land, beautiful dales and waterfalls, wild moors, Pennine heights, sandy bays and cliff lifts, ancient houses and abbeys, the spa towns of Harrogate and Scarborough, Pennine mill towns both large and small, canals, industrial museums and industrial cities, and the historic minster city of York. Yorkshire goes on and on. Perhaps this, as the American Henry Adams felt in 1906, accounts for Yorkshire's 'social independence of London . . . To a certain degree, evident enough to Yorkshiremen, Yorkshire was not English – or was all England, as they might choose to express it.'

Centuries earlier the Abbot of York in 1556 remarked, 'there be such a company of wilful gentlemen in Yorkshire as there be not in all England beside.' William Cobbett, in 1830, saw it another way. 'Yorkshiremen are looked upon

as being keener than other people; more sharp and more selfish . . . For my part . . . I always found Yorkshiremen distinguished for their frank manners and generous disposition . . . Everything they think soon gets to the tongue, and out it comes, heads and tails, as fast as they can pour it.' Whatever the truth of the matter, these 'wilful Yorkshire gentlemen' (and ladies) have over the years been responsible for, among other things, the charting of the east coast of Australia and numerous Pacific islands (Captain James Cook), the abolition of slavery in British lands (William Wilberforce), putting an end to the use of children for long hours in mills (Richard Oastler), free education for all British children (W. E. Forster), the Huddersfield Choral Society, and the Yorkshire County Cricket Club – members of which must have been born in Yorkshire. Last but not least they have given us Yorkshire pudding which, if served in the traditional manner, is eaten with onions and gravy before the meat course. What better way to start a journey through Yorkshire?

1 A peaceful, rural scene near Ilkley, West Yorkshire

NORTHERN YORKSHIRE

Stretching from the east Pennines to the North Sea, northern Yorkshire embraces the North York Moors National Park, the Yorkshire Dales, the splendid coastline from north of Whitby to south of Scarborough, and the city of York.

To visit York is to be conscious of history at every turn. It is a medieval city, built over and around a Roman one. The medieval walls, largely on the site of their Roman predecessors, still almost completely encircle the city and can be walked, giving excellent views of the minster and other historic buildings. The great gates that remain, such as Micklegate Bar and Bootham Bar, were built to prevent unwanted incursions, particularly from the north. The Roman streets are still there – Stonegate is built on the course of the Roman *Via Pretoria*, and Petergate on the *Via Principalis*. For three centuries York was the Romans'

headquarters for campaigns in the north. Constantine the Great was proclaimed Roman Emperor here. The Yorkshire Museum has a fascinating collection of Roman tombstones which show names from every corner of the Roman Empire. Artefacts dug up from all over York give a clear picture of everyday urban life.

The Viking legacy is present in the street names – gate, as in Stonegate, comes from the Danish *gata* for street, but it is possible to see, hear and smell what life in York was like in AD 948 at the Jorvik Viking Centre.

York Minster, built as we see it today between 1220 and 1472, is an architectural masterpiece. The Shambles, the Treasurer's House, the York Castle Museum, the Merchant Adventurers' Hall, and the narrow medieval streets and alleyways packed with fine shops and restaurants make York an excellent place to spend time in.

In complete contrast, the coastline of North Yorkshire has a wonderful landscape of collapsed cliffs as a result of the continual ravages of the North Sea, and supports a rich variety of plants, animals and birds. Many of the best views are only accessible on foot, but there are features for everyone to enjoy at Scarborough – cliffs, a castle, a harbour and lighthouse, parks, a funfair and a sandy beach with donkeys. Further north, in the peaceful little fishing village of Robin Hood's Bay, it is easy to forget how hard it was to make a living from the sea at the time when Captain James Cook set sail from Whitby to land at Botany Bay, Australia.

The North York Moors National Park encompasses heather moors, deep green dales and waterfalls, charming rural villages, Yorkshire's finest coastal areas, splendid monastic remains, and a 28-kilometre (18-mile) steam railway between Pickering and Grosmont. To the south of the Howardian Hills stands the noble edifice of Castle Howard. The long list of castles, historic houses and monastic ruins includes Richmond, Ripley and Skipton castles; Nunnington, Shandy and Beningborough halls; Selby, Rievaulx and Jervaulx abbeys and Mount Grace Priory. In the east is the Yorkshire Dales National Park. Swaledale, Wensleydale, Wharfedale and Ryedale are well known, but there are other dales waiting to be discovered by the visitor. They are all home to the sheep on which the prosperity of the great abbeys of the area was founded.

2 Tranquil Rosedale, once the scene of intense iron-mining activity

3 The North York Moors, near Hutton-le-Hole, which is one of the most attractive villages in the area

4 The North Yorkshire Moors Railway, between Pickering and Grosmont, runs through Goathland

5 The remains of Whitby Abbey overlook the fishing port of Whitby, which was one of the cradles of English Christianity

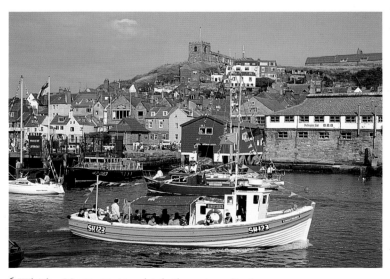

6 Whitby Museum, in which there is a display devoted to the Yorkshire-born navigator, Captain James Cook, is near the harbour

7 The whalebone at Whitby, signifying the past importance of this whaling port which is now a popular holiday resort

8 The Golden Ball Slipway at Scarborough, in the lively harbour area which has pleasant shopping streets, alleys and a cliff lift

9 The well-preserved fishing village of Robin Hood's Bay, to which access is on foot only, has spectacular views over a wide bay. Legend has it that Robin Hood fled here and disguised himself as a local fisherman to avoid arrest. The settlement has certainly been known by its present name since 1538

10 Charles Howard, third Earl of Carlisle, was responsible for the building of Castle Howard, the eighteenth-century palace designed by Sir John Vanbrugh and set on a hillside above a lake. It is possible to spend hours here visiting the costume display, the woodland garden, the lakes, the formal walled gardens, the Mausoleum and the Temple of the Four Winds

11 Ryedale Folk Museum is based in a collection of restored traditional buildings, which house exhibits and examples of local crafts

12 Rievaulx Abbey, built in the twelfth century, has some of the most majestic remains in the country

13 The Cistercian monastery which was founded in 1131 at Rievaulx ('valley of the Rye') is now in the care of English Heritage

14 As well as the spectacular setting of Rievaulx Abbey, there are parts of buildings or complete foundations for all the main rooms and outhouses showing how an abbey worked

15 Looking east down the nave of York's magnificent minster, on which building work started in about 1220

17 The Choir Screen in York Min[ster] has fifteen statues of kings of Eng[land] from William I to Henr[y]

18 It is possible to walk most of the way around York's medieval walls and gain excellent views of the city, dominated by the minster

16 The Shambles, York, gets its name from the 'shammels' (benches) on which the butchers' shops displayed their wares – nearly every shop was a butcher's until the 1930s

19 York Castle Museum has an authentic reconstruction of Victorian Kirkgate with various types of shop displays

20 Boat rides can be taken on the River Ouse from the Guildhall and under Lendal Bridge

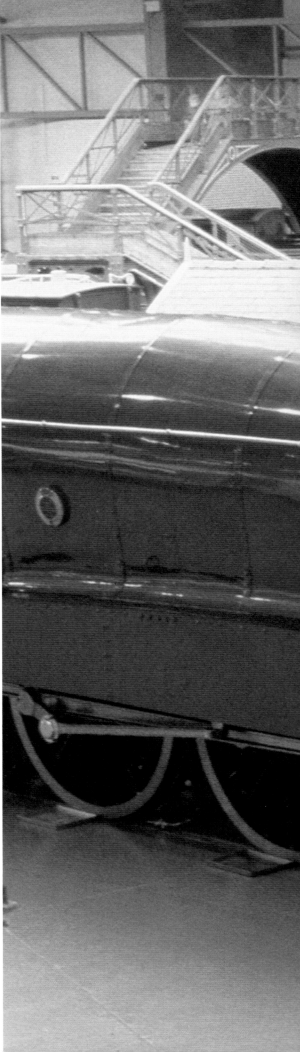

21 George Hudson, a local draper, made his fortune during the railway boom and made York an important railway centre. It is fitting that the National Railway Museum should be housed here

22 Montpellier Parade in Harrogate's attractive town centre, which boasts the best quality shops in Yorkshire

23 Valley Gardens, Harrogate, is a classic Victorian pleasure ground with ornamental gardens, boating pond, tearoom and Sun Colonnade

24 The octagonal Pump Room Museum is where the spa waters were first taken in Harrogate

25 A rural scene near Burnsall, one of the villages on the banks of the River Wharfe

26 The Moon Pond and Temple of Piety in Studley
Royal Park, which was laid out in the eighteenth
century and is now owned by the National Trust

27 Fountains Abbey, designated a World Heritage Site
and owned by the National Trust, is one of Yorkshire's
foremost beauty spots. Cistercian monks built it in 1132;
since the eighteenth century its ruins have provided a
dramatic backdrop for Studley Royal Park

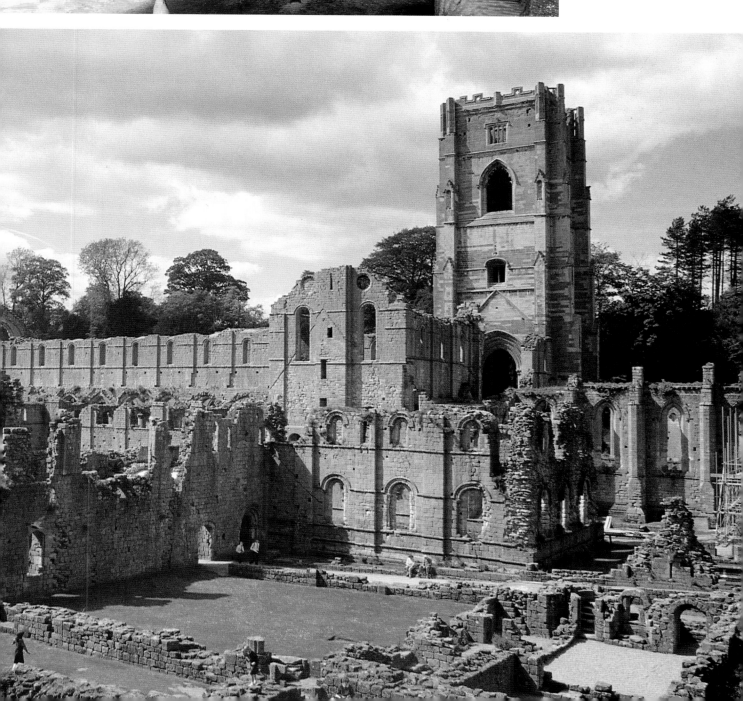

29 Upper Wharfedale Folk Museum in Grassington is housed in two early eighteenth-century cottages

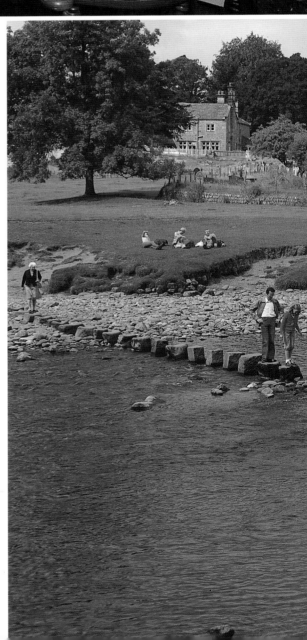

30 The fast-flowing River Wharfe at Linton is popular with fishermen

1 Augustinian canons built Bolton Abbey more than 800 years
go, as a priory. The dukes of Devonshire own the estate which,
aving open access, forms a gateway into the dales from the south

32 Malham Cove is a very popular place for mountaineers to practise their skills

33 This limestone pavement tops the sheer limestone cliff of Malham Cove

34 Malham Tarn, owned by the National Trust, is a wide, lonely expanse

5 The natural amphitheatre of Malham Cove is ne of the most spectacular sights in the dales

36 Three Peaks is the popular name for the three highest hills in the Yorkshire Dales – Pen-y-ghent (seen here), Ingleborough and Whernside. All three can be viewed from the railway line that runs along Upper Ribblesdale from Settle

37 Kilnsey Crag is 51 metres (170 feet) high with the largest overhang in the country

38 Langstrothdale Chase was an ancient hunting area, hence its name

39 Gunnerside was an important lead-mining community in the nineteenth century. Today, the village is a charming rural dales settlement with stone cottages, a village square, pub and tearooms, in a fine position between meadows sweeping down to the River Swale

40 Cotter Force, in Wensleydale, is one of the falls
that add a spectacular element to the dales scenery

41 Steep hillsides and moorlands criss-crossed by drystone
walls characterise the walking country around Arncliffe

42 The view towards Gayle, near Hawes, which claims to be the home of Wensleydale cheese

43 A glorious panorama down Swaledale above Muker, which is the most idyllic of Swaledale villages

WESTERN YORKSHIRE

The best of Victorian Britain can be found in western Yorkshire, where the excellent industrial museums, such as Bradford and Calderdale (at Halifax), make the most of the area's history. Some mills have been put to new uses – in Saltaire, for example, which was a 'factory village' built in the 1850s to house 2,500 workers, the main mill now houses the national collection of paintings by the Bradford-born artist, David Hockney. Some mills still do what they have always done, such as Britain's only surviving clog mill near Hebden Bridge.

The busiest town centres reveal traces of their Georgian and medieval predecessors, and the centre of Leeds will appeal to those who like Victorian architecture. Market towns like Ilkley and Otley were the centres of commerce until the Industrial Revolution brought the factories. Halifax managed to escape the bulldozing trend of the 1950s and '60s so that its splendid Piece Hall is still intact. The town's guillotine, in use in the seventeenth century, has a full-scale replica in Gibbet Street. It was used to punish the theft of cloth valued at $13\frac{1}{2}$d or more, and gave rise to the Vagrant's Litany: 'From Hull, Hell and Halifax, good Lord deliver us'. Halifax has moved with the times and is now the home of Britain's largest hands-on museum for children – Eureka.

Woollen cloth was made by hand in western Yorkshire cottages for hundreds of years until the end of the

eighteenth and beginning of the nineteenth centuries, when simple machines run on water-power were introduced. The abundance of flowing water helped small Pennine villages develop into mill towns, and terraces of stone cottages appeared, clinging to the hillsides. As more factories were built, workers had to be specially housed and the larger centres grew. Today there are bustling markets and mill shops supplying bargains in the heart of the textile-manufacturing country.

Industrial success brings wealth and this has provided us with historic stately homes to visit in western Yorkshire. The palatial splendour of Harewood House was built on a fortune made in the West Indies, and the Jacobean manor of East Riddlesden Hall was improved by a rich clothier from Halifax. There are many others, set in peaceful parkland even though they are close to the urban centres of Leeds, Huddersfield or Bradford.

Two of western Yorkshire's most popular places must be Haworth, home of the Brontës, and Holmfirth, featured in the television series, *Last of the Summer Wine*.

44 Near this country scene lies the busy mill town of Hebden Bridge

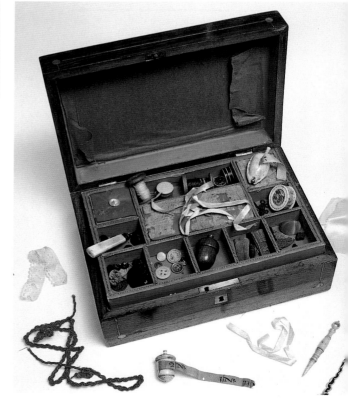

Haworth is the place to visit to see Brontë memorabilia.
The parsonage where the sisters lived (**45**) is now a
museum displaying their rooms and possessions (Patrick
Brontë's bedroom, **46**; Charlotte's workbox, **47**). The
Brontë Memorial Chapel (**49**) is in Haworth church (**48**)

50 Main Street in Haworth. Visitors from all over the world visit this small Pennine manufacturing town because of its association with the Brontës

51 A typical pair of the traditional
shops that line Main Street in Haworth

52 Haworth is still about the same size as it was when
the Brontës lived in it from 1820 to 1861. Its steep cobbled Main
Street links the church and parsonage in the old village at the
top of the hill, with the mill town in the valley below

53 Charlotte Brontë's friend, Mary Taylor, lived in Red House, Gomersal. The house (now a museum) is furnished as it was in the 1830s

54 Halifax Piece Hall has been described as one of Europe's finest eighteenth-century buildings. It was designed as a market for the great wool trade, with 315 rooms around a quadrangle for cloth-traders' displays

55 The weathervane on the Piece Hall, Halifax, pays tribute to the sheep on which the town's prosperity was built from the thirteenth century onwards

56 Shibden Hall gives an intimate picture of life in a prosperous household of the seventeenth and eighteenth centuries. Outside, the Folk Museum of West Yorkshire is arranged as an early nineteenth-century village

58 The four-storey Moorside mills are the home of Bradford Industrial Museum and Horses at Work, which is devoted to the city's industrial heritage. The transport gallery display Bradford-made vehicles, such as these Jowett

57 Cartwright Memorial Hall, in Lister Park, Bradford, houses the city's museum and art gallery. This splendid purpose-built gallery, with its flowing and exuberant Edwardian Baroque architecture, was opened in 1904. A new gallery of trans-cultural arts was recently opened, and there is a lively programme of temporary exhibitions.

59 In the nineteenth century Bradford was the 'worste capital' of the world; the Industrial Museum shows th machines which were used in cloth production and othe locally-made machines like this Carr Foster engin

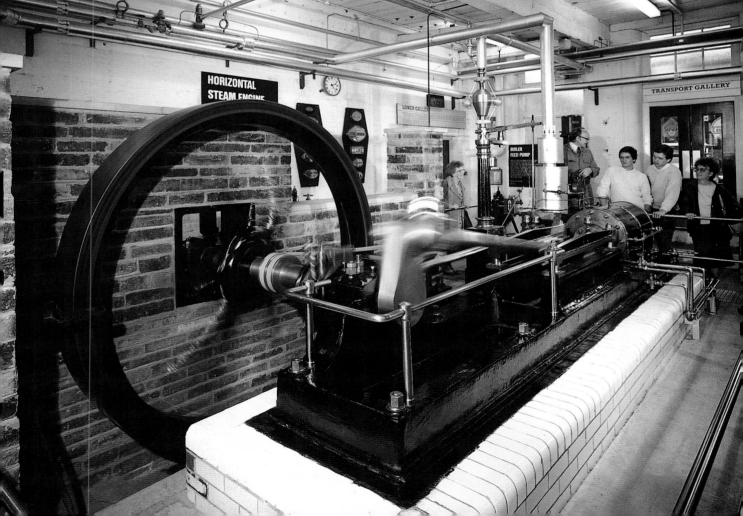

60 Most of Harewood House was built in the 1770s by the first Lord Harewood, who commissioned Robert Adams to design the interiors and Thomas Chippendale to make the furniture. Paintings, porcelain, ornate ceilings and rich wood carvings that look like taffeta pelmets contribute to the richness of its fabric and contents

61 Capability Brown landscaped the 1,000-acre park at Temple Newsam in the 1760s. It now includes seven gardens, a home farm with rare breeds of livestock, woodland and avenues. The house is a Tudor and Jacobean mansion

62, 64 Postcards became popular collectors' items after the Second World War and there is a fine exhibition in the Holmfirth Postcard Museum – including saucy seaside subjects even though the town is 128 kilometres (80 miles) from the sea

63 This house in Holmfirth belongs to the television character Nora Batty in the popular series, *Last of the Summer Wine*

65 A rooftop view of Holmfirth, an attractive town of narrow alleys, weavers' cottages and handsome old mills, dominated by an eighteenth-century church

66 A spinning jenny being demonstrated in the Colne Valley
Museum, in which working hand-looms incorporating the
flying-shuttle method are also shown. The museum, housed
in three nineteenth-century weavers' cottages, shows the
long-gone life and working world of local people

67 Byram Arcade is one of the pedestrianised areas in the shopping centre of Huddersfield, 'the fairest of all the English industrial towns', as Friedrick Engels described it. The local Ramsden family owned almost all of the town centre and planned it carefully

68 An old, narrow pack-horse bridge at Marsden, the last town before Lancashire. It is one of several textile towns that line the Pennine valley-bottoms and enhance the countryside with their stone walls

69 Tunnel End Canal and Countryside Centre at Marsden is based in what was formerly the tunnel-keeper's cottage. It has canal memorabilia and informative displays about the Pennine countryside. The towpath of the Marsden to Slaithwaite section of canal is ideal for walkers

70 The octagonal Wesleyan chapel at Heptonstall was
built in 1764. There is an excellent walk between
Heptonstall and Hebden Bridge, lower down the valley.
The route crosses a pack-horse bridge

71 An interior view of the octagonal Wesleyan chapel at Heptonstall, built in 1764. The poet Sylvia Plath is buried in the graveyard

73 Heptonstall Old Grammar School, an early seventeenth-century school building, is now a museum that tells the story of the village, which grew from a collection of stone weavers' cottages and crooked streets on a moorland ridge

2 Hebden Bridge, seen here from Heptonstall,
was the site of new textile mills when steam
power arrived. Terraces of weavers' cottages
were built at this time, crowding the hillsides

74 The four-storey houses in Hebden Bridge are divided in two; the top two floors are entered from the street above, the bottom two from the street below

75 Hardcastle Crags, 2.4 kilometres (1½ miles) from
Hebden Bridge, is also known as 'Little Switzerland'

76 Walks through the National Trust's Hardcastle Crags
go through woodland and beside Hebden Water

77 Canal trips are available at Hebden Bridge and ancient
cars may be hired at Automobilia in Old Town

SOUTHERN YORKSHIRE

Coal and other heavy industries are in decline here, with the result that the older southern Yorkshire is re-surfacing; green willows, shrubs and, in some places, fig trees line the River Don. The M1 passes through woods, by fields with deer browsing in them, and stately homes. Throughout southern Yorkshire, ancient copses and cornfields, poppy-red in early summer, can be seen.

Geographically, the area includes the southern Pennines to the west and part of the Peak District National Park; the centre is dominated by the coalfield, and the east boasts one of Britain's most important peat bogs, the wilderness of Thorne Moors. This is much more accessible than its Scottish counterparts and is at the centre of a great controversy about extraction for garden peat. In complete contrast, in the grounds of Cusworth Hall, near Doncaster, cedars, strawberry trees, larches, cypress, fig, yew and bamboo still flourish in the pleasure grounds of this excellent example of an early Georgian mansion. A museum illustrates life in South Yorkshire over the past 200 years. Conisbrough Castle is the setting for Sir Walter

Scott's *Ivanhoe*; English Heritage hold regular archery or sword-fighting contests in the courtyard, at which it is easy to imagine going back in history.

Sheffield is at the heart of southern Yorkshire. Built on seven hills, it is a busy modern city where the history of the steel-making industry, which earned the city a worldwide reputation, is displayed with pride. The diversity of the city's products: penny-farthing bicycles, lawn-mowers, silver-plated candelabra, steam engines, pocket watches and engineers' tools, are displayed in Sheffield Industrial Museum, which was a generating station in the nineteenth century. Not far away, the tiny rural workshops of Shepherd Wheel are a good example of the functional, straightforward industrial architecture of the eighteenth century.

78 The Worsbrough valley lake is flanked by the Liverpool-to-Hull footpath

79 The water-powered Worsbrough Mill Museum sells stoneground flour, made the way it has been for centuries

80 The Abbeydale Industrial Hamlet, Shef was one of the largest water-powered site forging scythes on the River Sheaf. The proc of making crucible steel for the scythes c seen; the grinding shop (left, **81**) and the forge (right, **82**) are just two examples c eighteenth-century works

83 Endcliffe Park is one of Sheffield's splendid parks for which it is justly praised

84 Sheffield city centre is the hub of a complex of first-rate museums, art galleries, theatres and self-employed craftsmen's premises

85 The friezes on the old Town Hall, Sheffield, depict the craftsmen, buffers, grinders and platers of the steel industry, for which the city is famous. The statue of Vulcan on the top, the Roman god of weapon-forging and ironmongery, is very appropriate

86 On one side of the seven hills of Sheffield are the Georgian houses of Paradise Square, where John Wesley often preached